POST TRAUMATIC PRESS 2007

in peace

poems by veterans

Collected by Dayl Wise
Copy editor, Alison Koffler

"...Above all I am not concerned with poetry. My subject is War, and the pity of war, the poetry is in the pity." - Wilfred Owen

Front cover photo: *Marine in Trench at Con Thien, Vietnam, 1967,* by David Douglas Duncan with permission from the Harry Ransom Humanities Research Center, The University of Texas at Austin.

Back cover photo: World War I memorial statue on Mosholu Parkway, Bronx NY, photo by D. Wise

Proceeds to Veterans for Peace

Post Traumatic Press 2007.
Copyright © 2007 by Dayl Wise
PTP, 104 Orchard Lane North, Woodstock, NY 12498
E- mail: dswbike@aol.com
Visit web site at PostTraumaticPress.org

Copy Editor: Alison Koffler, poet, teacher/consultant

Photo Consultant: John Huftalen, photographer

First Edition published June 2007
Second Edition, May 2008.
ISBN # 1-57256-08-0

POST TRAUMATIC PRESS 2007

poems by veterans

Collected by Dayl Wise
Copy editor, Alison Koffler

"...Above all I am not concerned with poetry. My subject is War, and the pity of war, the poetry is in the pity." - Wilfred Owen

Post Traumatic Press 2007.
Copyright © 2007 by Dayl Wise
PTP, 104 Orchard Lane North, Woodstock, NY 12498
E- mail: dswbike@aol.com
Visit web site at PostTraumaticPress.org

Copy Editor: Alison Koffler, poet, teacher/consultant

Photo Consultant: John Huftalen, photographer

First Edition published June 2007
Second Edition, May 2008.
ISBN # 1-57256-08-0

INTRODUCTION
By Dayl Wise

I have put this book together to tell the stories of veterans with direct experience of the military. For some, the intense experience of war can only be expressed in poetry, while others are driven by the need to say something openly political. This chapbook includes veterans from World War II, the Cold War, Korean War, Vietnam War, peace time and the current wars in Iraq and Afghanistan.

Thanks to the soldier-poet contributors: Camillo "Mac" Bica, Richard Boes, Thomas Brinson, Michael Embrich, Michael Gillen, Marc Levy, Bob Lusk, Gerald McCarthy, Jim Murphy, Fred Nagel, Ron Thompson, Robert "Tack" Trostle, Jose Vasquez, Jay Wenk, Dan Wilcox, Sam Weinreb and Larry Winters. Some of these US veterans are seasoned writers, who have been published before. For others, this is their first time writing, their first time out crossing that line in public. Check out those who have web pages, blogs, myspaces and contact them by e-mail.

All works are poems, songs, short stories or spoken word with the exception of chapter 10 of Richard Boes' book *The Last Dead Soldier Left Alive*. (The book is his personal experience, a first hand inquiry into why thousand of Vietnam Veterans have committed suicide.) Richard's book can be ordered through booksellers or by contacting:

Iuniverse
2021 Pine Lake Road, Suite 100
Lincoln, NE 68512
www.iuniverse.com
1.800.Authors (1.800.288.4677)

Larry Winters' book, *The Making and Un-making of a Marine*, is his life's journey, which includes as part of its central theme the Viet Nam War and his search for a role in the world after the war, can be purchased at his website makingandunmaking.com.

Gerald McCarthy's book, *Trouble Light*- a new full–length collection of his poetry- will be published by West End Press/University of New Mexico Press in 2008.

Special thanks to Alison Koffler, Sharon Morrison, Dan Wilcox, Richard Boes and Jim Murphy for supporting me in putting this collection together. And to Gerald McCarthy who in 1993 signed his poetry book *Shoetown* for me. He also wrote the words, "...*write it out*"! I took his advice.

CONTENTS

ACKNOWLEDGMENTS

Some works in this collection have been published previously.

Marc Levy
    poetz.com: (2006)   "AN OPEN DREAM TO RESIDENTS OF THE UNITED STATES"
    New Millennium Writings: "He Would Tell You"

Michael Embrich
    Helium.com: "I"

Larry Winters
    makingandunmaking.com: "Confession", "Vietnam" & "America"

Gerald McCarthy
    War.Literature: "Pylon" & "Winter Solstice"

Camillo "Mac" Bica, Ph.D., is a professor of philosophy at the School of Visual Arts in New York City. As a veteran recovering from his experiences as a United States Marine Corps officer during the Vietnam War, he founded, and coordinated for five years, the Veterans' Self-Help Initiative, a therapeutic community of veterans suffering from post traumatic stress disorder. He is a long-time activist for peace and justice, a member of Vietnam Veterans Against the War, and a founding member of the Long Island chapter of Veterans For Peace. Poems and articles by Dr. Bica have appeared in The Humanist Magazine, Znet, Truthout.com, Monthly Review Zine, Foreign Policy in Focus, and numerous philosophical journals.
E-mail: cbica@sva.edu
Web site: www.svaphilosopher.com

A Sign of the Times

A body of a dead VC sapper stands upright,
impaled in the layers of concertina wire
marking the no-man's land that surrounds
the perimeter of a firebase north of Danang.
Killed trying to penetrate the base's defenses,
his catatonic body adorned by holiday revellers,
with Christmas balls, tinsel, and a sign,
soiled with blood and entrails,
wishing all peace and good will
from Victor Charlie.
As we passed by and entered the base,
few even took notice.
I heard one young Marine,
nineteen years old and newly arrived in Country;
whisper to no one in particular.
"Ho, fucking ho, fucking ho."
We had grown indifferent to death and human suffering.
The innocence of youth dies quickly,
When killing becomes a rite of passage.

War Crazy

I have always thought myself a free spirit,
A philosopher mendicant,
seeking an alternative,
more substantive, lifestyle.
So many others, however, see my unorthodoxy,
my "spiritual seeking,"
as abnormal and a clear indication of my insanity.
Perhaps I need to pause and to reevaluate my life.
After all, being insane is not something one readily admits.
I guess it's part of being crazy
to cling to a facade of sanity,
to think oneself normal
and everyone else insane.

One thing I am certain of, however.
I haven't always been crazy.
Wasn't born crazy.
I think insanity crept up on me,
happened in Vietnam, in the war.
War does that, you know, drives people crazy.
Shell shock, battle fatigue,
soldier's heart, PTSD.
All that killing and dying can make anyone crazy.

Some survive war quite well, they tell me.
Many even benefit from its virtues.
But war's effects are not always apparent.
No one escapes war unscathed,
In body and in mind.
All war, any war, every war,
Ain't no virtue in war.

I think, of those not driven crazy by war,
many were crazy already.
But theirs was an insanity of a different kind,
a hard kind, an uncaring kind.
I knew people like that.
While I didn't like them much,
I thought them fortunate,
as killing and dying meant nothing.
In fact, in a perverse way, they enjoyed it,

enjoyed the jazz, the excitement, the power.
They became avenging angels, even god herself,
making decisions of life and death,
but mostly death.
Those crazies hated to see the war end.
For me, the war never ends.

Sometimes things work out for the best, though,
as my unorthodoxy, my being crazy,
probably saved my life.
You see, sane people can't live like this,
in a war that never ends.
Not all crazy people can either.
Guess I was lucky.
Sometimes being crazy helps you cope.
Sometimes, I wish I was crazier than I am.

Serious introspection has made clear
the foundations of my unorthodoxy,
the nature of my insanity.
It is a cruel wisdom
Allowing no better, compelling
a clarity of vision.
I have seen the horror of war,
the futility and the waste.
I have endured the hypocrisy and arrogance
of the influential and the wealthy,
and have tolerated the ignorance and narrow mindedness
of the compliant and the easily led.
War's malevolent benefactors,
who pretend and profess their patriotism
with bumper-sticker bravado,
with word but not deed,
intoxicated by war's hysteria,
from a safe distance.
Appreciative of our sacrifices they claim
as they applaud the impending slaughter,
sanctioning by word, or action, or non-action
sending other men and women
to be killed, and maimed,
and driven crazy by war.

And when they benefit from the carnage no longer,
their yellow ribbon patriotism
and shallow concern
fade quickly to apathy and indifference.
The living refuse of war that returns
are heroes no longer,
but outcasts and derelicts,
and burdens on the economy.
The dead, they mythologize with memorials
and speeches of past and future suffering
and loss.
Inspiring and prophetic words
by those who sanction the slaughter
to those who know nothing of sacrifice.

I used to try to explain war
to help them understand and to know its horror,
naively believing that war was a deficiency,
of information, understanding,
discernment, and vision.
But being crazy has liberated me
allowing me to see that war is not a deficiency at all,
but an excess, of greed, ambition, intolerance,
and lust for power.
And we are its instruments, the cannon fodder,
expendable commodities in the ruthless pursuit
of wealth, power, hegemony, and empire.

And now, I accept and celebrate my unorthodoxy,
my insanity, as an indictment
of the hypocrites and the arrogant,
of the ignorant and the narrow-minded
for a collective responsibility and guilt
for murder and mayhem,
and crimes against humanity.
And I offer my insanity as a presage
of their future accountability,
to humankind in the courts of history,
and to the god they invoke so often
to sanction and make credible
their sacrilege of war.

The Centurion

Concertina, tanglefoot, trip flares,
pebble filled beer cans, and claymores.
81 mike mikes delivering daylight upon command,
used sparingly so as not to compromise our position.
As though they didn't know.

Sensing devices, listening posts, and starlight scopes
providing eyes that penetrate the darkness.
360 perimeter integrity, sectors of fire overlapping,
with the 60s standing ready
to saturate the likely avenues of approach.

M79s and LAWs for added firepower
and to cover any deadspace the terrain may impose.
Reserves in secondary positions
to respond to sapper penetration,
with the COM established
to coordinate and control the entire fiasco.

PRC25s, FDC, and azimuths,
with pre-registered targets
for quick and accurate H.E. and W.P.,
air bursts my favorite.
Phantoms and Puff
providing a downpour of nap and steel,
with red smoke to pinpoint the inferno.

Strategy to match the brilliance of Caesar.
But this is not the Gallic wars.
Does Charlie appreciate such tactical genius?
How could he, for we are the noble legions
and he the ignorant barbarian.

The board has been set, and, like pawns,
we await his next maneuver.
Ghostly shadows, silently probing and sniping,
hoping to fund a vulnerable jugular.

Endless nights, limitless horror,
and senseless deaths.

High school dropout men of medicine,
clumsily restoring bowels to mutilated abdominal cavities,
while muffling the screams of unbearable pain and horror,
with injections of morphine and empty promises of tomorrow.

Body bags, toe tags, and medevacs to graves registration.
Military escorts, flag draped-coffins
and devastated loved ones,
comforted only by a seven gun salute
initiating the trumpeter's final farewell.
Patriotism, nationalism, and Communism,
the angry gods of archaic religions
all demanding appeasement through human sacrifice.
. . . I've become an atheist.

Memories, daydreams, and nightmares
my constant companion
as I await the merciful dagger of Brutus.

Star light Star bright

The night holds no secrets from me.
For I have the power to see
into its most impenetrable shadows.
I have become like the owl,
a most proficient predator,
sitting patiently upon my carefully chosen roost
silently awaiting my prey.

Hoo, Hoo. It's what I do.
It's neither right, nor is it wrong.
For such judgments mean nothing to me.
For this is a wild place,
a place of predator and prey.
So I wait, and nothing shall escape my cunning.
The shadows can offer no sanctuary,
for my steady, callous glance
can penetrate even the darkest of hiding places.

My prey shall have no warning,
nor will he see or hear his death swoop down upon him.
And then for an instant, he will know the horror
as he feels the steel of my talons penetrate his skin.
And when the ritualistic feast is over,
I return to my roost, still savoring a final bit of entrail.
Hoo, Hoo, it's what I do.

Richard Boes enlisted into the US Army and served in Vietnam in 1969 - 1970 with the First Air Cav. His book, *The Last Dead Soldier Left Alive* is his personal experiential account; a first hand inquiry into why thousands of Vietnam Veterans have committed suicide. He lives alone in upstate New York, in an apartment he deems a glorified bunker.

The Wall

Chapter Ten of *The Last Dead Soldier Left Alive*

I don't want to be doin' this anymore. I'm sick to death of my own story, but there's only one way out. I'm up against the outer Wall motherfucker! I'm unstoppable.

. . .

I went to all kinds of meetings, Al-Anon, CoDA, Adult Children of Alcoholics, read whatever self-help books, books about trauma, the Bible front to back, each chapter three times, even went to church on Sundays, sometimes during the week. Still, I hadn't a clue, an inkling who or what might fix me. Ann suggested a twelve-week residential program for PTSD, (post traumatic stress disorder). It was all I'd left to try, but I'd have to wait a few weeks. In the interim, James thought it might do me some good to visit the Wall, he'd even pay for the trip. I'd left my parents' home a month earlier, had stopped working altogether, it was getting harder to leave my room, I'd count the cars from the trucks passin' without looking, without leaving my bed. James was HIV-positive, I thought I might be of some assistance, moved in with him up north, a country postcard kind of town with a tiny train station, a secret underground passage, and big old oak trees whose leaves were in flame. James was afraid he'd never see them leaves again. Even though we routinely shared needles I somehow missed the virus both he and Bubba caught.

I'd never been to the Wall before. It was Veterans Day 1993. I made the trip with Patrick, a sober vet, I'd known from

city meetings. We didn't know each other that well, but this trip would change all that. He was fuckin' nuts, had a bull's-eye tattooed on the back of his bald head, didn't want them to miss. "They just want us dead!" we told each other repeatedly, we'd served our purpose. Me too, I guess, I was fuckin' nuts. It was the year they were dedicating a statue commemorating the women who'd served in Vietnam. We drove down the day before, spent the night at a Holiday Inn.

We were both up at five, smoking cigarettes, drinking coffee, and writing in our journals. There seemed no difference between us, we were both on edge, anxious, and shared the same demons.

We got to the Wall about 7:00 A.M., no crowds yet, people were just beginning to arrive. I wore a First Cav pin, and everyone I saw with a First Cav pin or patch, I'd ask what company they were with; I was desperately looking for someone I knew. "Welcome home, welcome home, welcome home," was all anyone said like I'd just arrived, come home, assuming, I did come back.

"If!"

"Yeah," was my only response. As the day wore on I became that much more desperate. Patrick, too. The situation only got worse, hopeless, futile, all these soldiers, and nobody I knew. Where the fuck was Myles, anyway?

Our first trip along the Wall, that longest walk, I found the names, saw the faces of ghosts, Rodney C. Brown, I ran my fingers over, over and again, over the groves, "If!" Bounce, bouncin' Betty, fuckin' B-40! Buttkins, Henderson, Walsh, Casey fuckin' Jones, but they left out the *fuckin'*. Patrick's name was on the Wall with a different middle initial. I knew what the fuck he was thinkin', 'If!'"

It occurred to me that other names were missing-O'Brien,

Smyth, Uncle Joe, Charlie, thousand of others, hadn't their suicides been motivated by the war, hadn't the war killed them too? I had an idea, they should build an outer Wall about twenty-five yards from this existing Wall, encircling it with the names of the post war fallen. Might there be twice, or thrice as many names? You'd have to walk the path between the Walls, from side to side, and ghosts be snappin' at your heels, picking your brain. You'd have to ask yourself why? What part did you play, or not play, how had you contributed to this tragic fuckin' mess! Again I thought, we were all wrong.

Each pass we made along the Wall, the greater the crowds, the more things left behind, boots, wineglasses, photographs, letters, children's drawings, tarnished medals, all that remained the same were the names, you couldn't change that. I kept askin', but there was no one, no one I knew had been left alive. Truly, truly I believed, Jesus, I must be the last dead soldier still breathing.

As the parade entered the grounds and began to disperse, about three hundred of us guys, all Vietnam vets, made a path for the women to pass through, wheelchairs parted, canes saluted, we were all applauding, "Thank you, thank you, thank you," I kept saying over, over and again, I was crying, it was somethin' no one had ever said to me. One kind nurse with angelic features, back lit and haloed, broke file, came over and gave me a hug, this started Patrick cryin' too.

The unveiling of the statue was to take place later that afternoon. We kept walking around, circlin' the grounds, thousands of people doin' the same thing too, like one giant fuckin' merry-go-round. That ride always made me fuckin' sick. "Welcome home, welcome home, welcome home." Shut up already! I just kept seein' the same ghostly faces, the same faded green fatigues, the same patches, ribbons, and purple hearts, over, over and again, and nobody I knew. I finally realized with sudden impact like runnin' smack

damn into a Wall, that I wasn't looking for someone I knew. NO! But for that part of me I'd lost. And thousands of others like war trolls were doin' the same thing too, but most of 'em didn't know it. And all these POW-MIA flags, we are the prisoners, missing in action. And up against the outer Wall motherfuckers!

Simultaneously, Patrick and I turned to each other with a simple request, "Let's leave." We never did stay for the ceremonies.

. . .

Later that month, at my twenty-fifth year high-school reunion, after eight years, nine months, and twenty-seven days of sobriety, I got fuckin' drunk!

Thomas Brinson currently serves as a facilitator for Chapter 138 of Long Island Veterans For Peace, and as the Long Island contact for Vietnam Veterans Against The War. He served in the II Corps Vietnam from 1967 to 1968, and as a Peacemaker on the Nonviolent Peaceforce in Mutur, Trincomalee, Sri Lanka from 2003 to 2005. www.livfp.active.ws

chant

Buddhist monks
in nearby monastery
drone atonal chant
through darkest moments
before dawn

I sit and watch
fall of gentle rain
streetlight shimmer upon waving fronds
sleeping cat startles itself awake
then slinks away in shadows

Distant rumble of rolling sound
thunder, or mortars of LTTE attack?
flash of lightning brings memory
of jungle war of long gone youth

I swat at whining buzz of mosquito
again lose count of breaths
another blessing to extend forgiveness
starting with myself

Such is my life
as I pray
not to judge it too harshly
instead to smile a mantra
of gratitude for mere
magnificent being

December 13, 2004, Dambulla, Sri Lanka

Walking the line in Phoenix...

A cool desert sun bore down
upon this palm-treed metropolis
where the streets were mostly empty
except for the gentle gathering
of us alarmed, concerned citizenry
marching in massed dissent
to protest once more one other
unjust, illicit, unnecessary war
threatening our post-post modern age

Also in the streets were stern protectors of the law
ordered minions of the virulent police state
riot troops in menacing full battledress regalia
dark blue uniforms and jack boots
large billy clubs and gas masks
helmeted Plexiglas masks and shields
forming two impenetrable lines
flanked by a phalanx of mounted police
slowly squeezing the rag-tag militia
of chanting, dancing, full-life-loving people
off the streets where they were cavorting
celebrating what real democracy looks like

A sudden thought struck me
it has been decades – 35 years in fact
since I had walked the line,
checking the troops, giving them heart
those mostly 18 & 19 year olds
from the wide countryside and ghettos
soldiers of the platoon I commanded
during brutal Tet of '68 in far-off Vietnam

So, following the impulse
impervious to personal peril
I stepped off the safety of the curb
to smartly walk the two ranks of line
stopping in front of each riot police trooper
to meet each pair of eyes, smiling widely
noticing them notice me, our common humanity
silently exhorting each one to kindly wage peace

February 16, 2003, Tucson, AZ

chief nurse

bleached hair

strands wispy

limply fall about

flushed eyes

running mascara

bluing the bright face

with the ready smile

which when curved wide

somewhat hides

the wrinkles

of a body

ounce-spreading

though still

supple-seeming

here in flare-flickering shadows

of frantic basecamp officers club

while pouring can after can of San Miguel

down my unquenchable throat

i imagine her name is marge

the fancy tonight of some colonel who buys drinks

and sneers while jerkily dancing

with a rather crooked beak

of one who leads desks and/or diagrams

the pity of it is

when young she probably loved children

maybe wanted one or ten

now she can only watch

them mutilated die

her surrogate sons

of my generation

by blistering day

she garbs herself

with scissors and gauze

stuck in pockets

of jungle fatigues

to guide those

younger than she

the nurses

who tend their would-be lovers

lost in this would-be war

Summer, 1967, Qui Nhon, Vietnam

stark memory

you looked up at me

with the precise peculiarity

of your smile

touching me

with a distinct embrace

my hand trembled

upon the round smallness

of your soft breast

the flesh quickening

with slight quivers

i knew then

i would remember you

in some place far-off

alien and strange

now

in this early morning light

drowsily munching stale c-rats

i am comforted

by your stark memory

gazing at silhouettes

of shredded viet cong

dangling mute

in concertina wire

March, 1968, Long My, Vietnam

valentine's day--1968

dust cakes into pores loosened by streams of sweat
the back and butt rebel at each rutted jolt
eyes tear with irritation and grime

fear like a tickling dream
scurries wetly about in gut

i gaze up the steep barren-stumped cliffs
below which are scattered about
like carcasses of dried locusts
debris of other war machines that didn't make it
as we wind a snail's pace way up
somewhere beyond the far ridge line

behind me
a grinding rev-straining
deuce-and-a-half
filled with crates of 105 ammo
presents of death for sir charles
on this valentine's day
lumbers through the dust
trailing after my gun-jeep

i wait watching i wait
listening jerkily all
around for swish
of rockets plop
of mortars thud
of grenades whine of
bullets the terrible
swift suddenness of
one mine which
others missed

flitting visions pass the mind in quick revolutions:
  --a girl baby tiny and cuddled cooing
  --one woman young lonely and fretting
  --parents stoically speaking to a uniformed stranger
  --sisters huddled around a flag-draped closed coffin
  --a mumbled plea for some god to maybe forgive

--the disturbing perfectly sane query
WHAT THE HELL AM I DOING HERE???

for small comfort is one meager carbine grasped more tightly

February 14, 1968, Pleiku, Vietnam

patriotic pondering

fact:

i was born

in a certain place

within a particular country

but that happenstance alone

is not enough - - no it doesn't suffice

to induce in me peacocked pride

stirring loyalty or blind patriotism

indeed

somewhat thankful

am i for it

now i serve it

in a war-torn land

distant and strange and unnecessary

where i just might die for it

or so the newspapers shall say

gallantly waxing trite rhetoric and hollow pomp

i'll just be dead - - small comfort for my next-of-kin

soon i may return to it

and maybe be happy in it

for awhile

but that won't make me stay

i very well may leave it

not quite ready yet

to fully accept

to be definitively sure

that some other place

other than it

far-off or near

isn't greater better

or more relevant

Somewhere in Vietnam.

Sometime during 1967-68.

one precious event

in this deep-dusk silence

of jungle-muted sounds

as the waning sun

disappears behind

orange-purple cloud-streaks

making shadows sharp

on the ragged ridges

of distant horizon

the heart-startling

hazards of day

are forgotten

and the soul

takes stock

pauses

for a moment

in the midst

of man-made inanity

to contemplate

precious events

those before

those hereafter

even those here

amid splintered chaos

like

the beer-bellied

cigar-mouthed tough

seasoned sergeant

bending a calloused

tender hand

to apply so gently

medicine

to the wound

of an ailing child

a victim of circumstance

and war

Sometime in 1967, Qui Nhon, Vietnam

Michael Embrich was raised in Jersey City, New Jersey. Upon graduating from Bayonne High School in June of 2000, Michael had a few choices. He was a gifted athlete and a good student. Michael elected to join the United States Navy in August 2000 and was stationed on board the USS Theodore Roosevelt (CVN-71). After the terrorist attacks on 9-11, Michael was deployed to the Indian Ocean and was a part of the initial combat strikes on the Taliban. After spending nine months in the theater, Michael returned home. His homecoming didn't last long because less than six months later he was deployed to the Mediterranean Sea to take part in initial combat operations on Saddam Hussein's Iraqi military. Michael returned home six months later and shortly after he was honorably discharged from the military. Michael currently resides in Bayonne, New Jersey and is majoring in history at Rutgers University. He is an avid human rights and anti-war advocate who enjoys writing, astronomy and philosophy. Michael has appeared on many political and news television programs and is currently working with the United States Senate on ways to end the war and provide support for the troops upon their return from war. Michael states, "You can learn a great deal about mankind when you come to the realization that the greatest, most innovative invention mankind has created was designed to destroy mankind."
E-mail: MichaelEmbrich@Gmail.com
myspace.com/michaelembrich

Iraq (A Poem)

No Salvation for the damned
No feast for the poor
It seems a long way from heaven in this desert,
I deplore
I spend little time smiling due to carrion
I inure
As we march we recite
No salvation for the damned
No feast for the poor

I

I lie awake, I see the sky
I,
Think of you
I
Wonder why
I
Want to touch you, feel you, smell you
I
want to hold you, want to tell you
I
Strive to live
I
Live to strive
I
May not make it home alive
I
Love you many miles away
I
Love you tomorrow, love you today
I
Lie awake
I
See the sky
I
Hope you still love me
I
Wonder why
I heard about him
Is it true?
Did you do?
What you said you wouldn't do
You
Lie awake
You

See the sky
You touch his cheek
You
Look in his eyes
you
Want to touch him, feel him, smell him
But there is one thing you just can't tell him
I
Lie awake,
I
See the sky
I

Michael Gillen entered the Merchant Marine in 1967, with Vietnam service in 1969. He teaches Asian History at Pace University in Pleasantville, New York, and a course on the Vietnam War at Purchase College, State University of New York. He is an active member of Vietnam Veterans Against the War and Veterans for Peace, chapter 60 in Westchester/ Rockland, New York. He lives in White Plains, New York. mgillen@pace.edu

Forced March
(From the American Civil War)

Slogging through mud,
tired and numb,
intent on reaching the battlefield in time,
the soldiers plod on.

Heads lowered in fatigue,
watching the worn heels
of the next soldier ahead,
they plod on, and on.

Many sleep as they march,
kept in line by an occasional bump,
through the long night,
on and on.

The silence of night
will soon give way,
to exhortations and screams,
cannon fire, and the clash of arms.

Through the night they march,
not long departed from camp,
and their mother's wombs,
to reach the killing field in time.

1980

These Years Later

It wasn't much: some weeks
riding shotgun over ocean blue
as bombs rested quietly below
us, in holds tight with dunnage.
Then more sitting, waiting, until
ROK stevedores worked us over,
and ship rose ever so slowly,
day after day, as war raged around
us, but still seemingly far away.
Phantoms screamed overhead,
choppers rose slowly off the deck
of a carrier, launches came and
went, disgorging seamen ashore.
And another ship burned away
that one night, after catching
rockets in wrong place, wrong
time, until it ceased to be living.
And then we steamed away,
weeks more until it was all
far, and years behind, us.
And now, as years turn to
decades, they're still clearly
there, those days of war.

2007

The Patrol Boat

Dawn...
Leaning on the ship's rail,
I watch the patrol boat
move off, leaving its trail
of dead fish as they float
by in the warm waters of the bay
(concussion grenades, dropped all night,
having kept VC swimmers away).
And in the sun later they'll bloat,
as the sun rises on another day
in the War Zone.

Marc Levy served as an infantry medic with the First Cavalry
in Vietnam and Cambodia in 1970. He was decorated once for
gallantry, twice for valor, and twice court-martialed. His work has
been published in various online and print journals, most recently in
Slowtrains, CounterPunch, and *New Millennium Writings.*

He Would Tell You

Here in the secret chambers
Of my darkest heart are things
I will never tell:
Here is oily blood and brittle bone
Here are clotted lips, frothy lungs
Decomposed and muted tongues
Here twisted cloth lays strangely stiff
In a powdery triptych pit
Where a dumbstruck man and wife
Lock quick lime arms round their
Dream face child, here
Past the graveyard's fragrant stones
Memory's nightmare head will not lay prone
Its battlefields etched on a red brocade
Inlaid with a crown of skull and bones
Yes, here in the busy chambers of my
Heart are things I will never tell
Though I swear we did not mutilate-
Only booby trapped or ransacked-
Disdained from taking human souvenirs.
No, we did not do that.
So, though I nearly did
Let me never tell you
Things you cannot know
Let me never tell you
Things that won't let go.

An Open Dream To Residents of The United States

I dreamed I was a perfect smile in a rainbow of fabulous babies. Each fabulous baby had three shot guns and their heads were made of papier-mache. When they spoke each baby fired a shot, then burped loud and far. The burps and shots alternated between rapid and slow speed. Each baby was fabulous because each resembled Liberace in perfect detail, from their rhinestone sequined diapers to their thick full hair, swept back like wire cables dipped in shiny hot tar.

Each rainbow baby spoke two hundred languages. Their bright pink mouths moved at the speed of light. A chorus of smoke and fiery words filled the cloudless sky. The babies were shooting and talking and burping straight up into the sun. Thunder and lighting boomed and flashed. The babies, illuminated by the lightning became silent and still. None burped or shot or spoke a foreign word. The teeth in my mouth became hollow. They clanged like glass bells.

A tall man in a long wood boat waved as he passed under the rainbow bridge. He spoke with a lisp and had magnificent jug ears.

"I'm from Cawfed, Tek-this," he said. "Ya'll thop your thooting so I can get thom thleep."

In the dream a single file of naked women eating handfuls of Nilla Wafers marched forward and surrounded the babies. The naked ladies marched and chewed and their dry contracting throats made a sound like wind through willows. This went on for quite some time.

Then one baby burped. Then another and another until their magnificent unified roar made all the flowers in the world droop and the naked ladies dropped their wafers and stopped chewing and begged the babies to stop.

Three babies stopped but the rest continued and the women retreated, running backwards, single file, swinging their arms, wiggling their fingers, and clearing their throats like quacking ducks. The magnificent babies jumped up and down, higher and higher. They grew long frizzy beards. They shaved them off. Now each baby looked exactly like Steve McQueen.

A giant bald eagle swooped down and attacked the babies, who fought back, hitting the swift flying bird with big puffy bags of one, five, and ten dollar bills. Afterwards, the babies emptied the bags of money over a cliff. Millions of dollars fluttered like snowflakes as they melted into the sea.

"Thank you thow much," said the man from Texas. "Thow vewy, vewy much."

Bob Lusk, a is a Hudson Valley, NY folksinger who plays a variety of Americana, Old Tyme, Country, Celtic, Anglo, Blues, and Spiritual music. His songs reflect a strong social conscience and a lifetime of working for peace, justice and social action. He frequently performs for movements for social change and is a member of Veterans For Peace.

When not performing professionally, he is frequently on the line at demonstrations with his banjo, brightening the spirits of the anti-war troops.

He is one of the "Kings Mall Seven," a group of veterans involved in a freedom of speech case, arrested for reading the names of soldiers who have died in the Iraq war outside of a recruiting station.
Web Site: http://www.boblusk.net

Read Me the Dead

Every Saturday morning Jay, David and Joan
Stand by the door, at the Kings' Mall
Outside the recruiters, they do their duty
They stand and recite the names of the dead.

Chorus:

Read me the dead, what were their names
Do you think this is some sort of game?
Read me the dead, what were their names
Do you think this is some sort of game?

That was my son, my daughter or brother
Uncle or aunt, friend or a lover.
Why did they go, what did they hope for?
Why are we here, who wants to know?

Chorus:

Cursed be the leaders, who shamed the memories
Of foot soldiers, veterans, each one a hero
These are their names, their battles have ended
We stand in their honor, we stand here for peace!

Chorus:

2006

OM

In Fort Dix, New Jersey, as in most military bases, there is a parade ground, sometimes used for parades (Which may be fun to watch, but are hell to be a part of). In the summer of 1967, several non-military type GIs including myself, would sit in a circle on the parade ground, chanting the OM mantra, watching the planes take off from Stewart Air Force Base.

As the planes would go from the extreme right to left, hugging the horizon and gaining altitude slowly, we would chant:

OM - - - - - - - -
OM - - - - - - -
OM - - - - - - -
OM - - - - - - -
"There it is - looks small," I would think to myself.
OM - - - - - - -
OM - - - - - - -
"A little plane in the sky"
OM - - - - - - -
OM - - - - - - -
"It flies so high"
OM - - - - - - -
OM - - - - - - -
OM - - - - - - -
"Carries troops, carries death"
OM - - - - - - -
"It flies the wind, but kills the breath"
OM - - - - - - - -
OM - - - - - - -
OM - - - - - - -
"Somewhere off in Vietnam"
OM - - - - - - -
"There flies your brother, dropping bombs"

OM - - - - - - -
OM - - - - - - -
OM - - - - - - -
1975

FORT DIX STOCKADE
Words: Bob Lusk   Tune: Columbus Stockade

I was in the Fort Dix, New Jersey, stockade from September 1967 to February 1968 because I refused to serve in Vietnam. I wrote this song in 1980 when I was playing with the Irish Bluegrass group 'The Green Ridge Boys'. The original stockade has now been demolished.

Over there, in Fort Dix, New Jersey
That's where I don't want to be
Over there, in that old stockade
Take me back to New York City

Chorus:
Oh you can take me back to Brooklyn
The Bronx or the Queens will be fine
Just turn me loose from this old stockade
I tell you buddy I won't mind

Late last night, as I lay sleeping
I dreamed I held you in my arms
When I awoke I was mistaken
Please keep my darling safe from harm

I don't want to cross the ocean
Don't want to fight any rich man's war
But if I ever leave this stockade
Ain't never comin' back no more

Well talk about the food,
Buddy, we don't get half enough
And the guards, they treat you mean boys
I tell you buddy, it's sure rough

1980

Gerald McCarthy is a member of Veterans for Peace, Chapter 60, Tappan Zee Brigade and Vietnam Veterans Against the War. His poems have been selected for inclusion in *Hawaii Pacific Review's* Best of the Decade issue and in *Twenty Years of Writing from Italian Americana*. New poems also appear in *The North American Review, War Literature & the Arts, Encounter*, and *White Pelican Review*. Trouble Light- a new full–length collection of his poetry- will be published by West End Press/ University of New Mexico Press in 2008. He served as a panelist for this year's New York Foundation on the Arts Poetry Fellowship competition. He lives in Nyack, New York with his wife Michele and their three sons Nick, Ben and Nate.

Pylon

And the young ones?
In the coffins
      Miguel Hernandez

At night, invisible
aluminum boxes
slide down steel rollers
out of the belly of a plane.

Names from a new wall
count off a kind of cadence,
marking time
no one hears.

Trucks wait to upload
their cargo.
Shadows edge the airstrip,
a greasy rain begins to fall.

Winter Solstice 2005 (or The New War Dead)

A flock of starlings
scuttle on the rooftop
splashing in pools of rainwater.

The last leaves in the branches
of the red maple tree.

Look, my friend says
there's a kind of dark
all around us,
you have to get used to it, s'all.

Bricker's neighbor shot himself in his garage,
the summer I turned eleven.
He drove an old gray Plymouth,
a car with a single headlight like a beak.
Birdman of Church Street, we called him.
The car was pulled in when the shot went off.
A pistol, Tommy said, Smith & Wesson 38.
Once in winter I cut the yards,
saw him bent over his workbench–
the trouble light overhead,
cigarette smoke.
He saw my shadow and looked up.

Now December rain keeps falling
and the news slips out.
The dead come back.
A line of graying birds
are huddled together in the rain.

The Wounded

There's a kind of dark that comes quietly
out on the edge of a field
so that when you look up, it's like a border
only fluid, moving.
A line of wild turkeys are feeding
on the grassy slope below the hill
near the entrance to what the locals call
the other Arlington – a hillside cemetery
off the old King's Highway,
and that darkness is coming toward them
out of the field's edge.
They keep feeding on the juniper
and bearberries,
circling one another,
a kind of grace in motion,
these birds blending into the shadows
of the March dusk.
If you listen you can hear
the soft clucking sounds they make
as the night keeps on.
Today in the glare of the super market
fluorescent light
my son makes me look at lobsters in their tank.
They don't move much in there, he says.
They're stunned, I tell him,
their claws taped up, waiting.
Outside in the cool night air
cold rain on stone—
you think of them, the wounded
trapped in their tanks
or hospital beds, dark shadows
that hang on the edge of dusk.

On a line by Li Po

Second snow of November,
already the high peaks are white
in the blue distance.

Now when I think of my first
homecoming,
I see myself bent double
carrying duffels down from a train–
city lights,
the war far away.

Tonight, my sons stand beside me
watching the fire.

A great horned owl's cry
pierces the dark, and I think
of what ruins our lives.

Jim Murphy is a USAF veteran, who served in Vietnam in 1967 and 1968 with the 1stMOB/1972nd in I Corps. Jim is a member of Vietnam Veterans Against the War, Veterans for Peace and is the coordinator of New York Veterans Speak Out…On War based in NYC. (www.veteransforpeaceny.org) An educator, Jim is retired as Dean of West Side High School in Manhattan and is currently F-status for the New York City Department of Education. He lives in Nyack, New York with his wife Susan, a film maker and educator, and two golden retrievers, Ceili and Seamus. They are empty nesters, with their son Corey off in school at SUNY Potsdam in upstate New York.
myspace.com/nycmurph -
E-mail: mandm11@optonline.net

I'm A FNP…. A Fuckin' New Poet

I just got in-poet-country….

These brothers have been here,

writing for a while….

Note how they keep their distance from me….

Not making attachments to me,

no eye contact…

FNP's are often killed or wounded

during the first 30 poems…

They don't want to put their poetry at risk

by being too close to me….

If I survive,

they'll look out for me…

I understand…

It's the code.

FNP is a direct reference to the slang FNG: most common name for newly arrived person in Vietnam. It was literally translated as a "Fuckin' New Guy" (or Girl).

Black Granite Panel 53W, Row 13

Full Name:	ALEXANDER ANTHONY ROCZEN
Wall Name:	ALEXANDER A ROCZEN
Date of Birth:	5/16/1947
Date of Casualty:	7/4/1968
Home of Record:	FAIRPORT
State:	New York
Branch of Service:	US Army; Co. A, 1st Bn., 8th Brigade, 4th Inf. Division
Rank:	PFC
Casualty Country:	SOUTH VIETNAM
Casualty Province:	KONTUM

The wall doesn't tell us about his parents,
his twin sister Alexandria;
a younger sister Nancy and a brother Kenneth...
a mother who grieves to this day...
his father, a decorated WW II hero
who never forgave himself....

That he had freckles,
a big gap in his front top teeth,
that he wasted his money trying to shave,
that he had a really goofy smile...
that when we caddied he always got the 30 handicap that followed a
slice with a hook...
and on the football field he was the gutsiest,
his uniform the dirtiest.

The record doesn't tell us that he wasn't even in-country a month...
in the service barely 6 months.

And 41 other guys died on July 4th 1968.

My Students Learn From You Kiki...

I tell your story every year to remind my students that life is precious and to make sure they treat everyone around them with love and respect. I tell them that you were a special kid who always had a smile and a good word. I tell them you were the lightest lineman I ever saw but that you made up for it in heart.

I miss you still...

Rest in peace, little brother...

> Left at the "Wall" by: Jim Murphy
> Relationship: Buddy
> 1st MOB Vietnam '68
> Tuesday, September 3, 2002

Fred Nagel is a vet (Korea in 1967-68) living in Rhinebeck, New York. Retired from Vassar College in 2002, Fred is involved in a number of progressive groups in the Hudson Valley: The Dutchess Greens, the Dutchess Peace Coalition, the Mid-Hudson Sister City Project, Northeast Citizens for Responsible Media, and the Middle East Crisis Response. Along with helping plan events for these organizations, Fred maintains their webpages. Fred is a DJ on WVKR, 91.3 FM, and his program, Activist Radio, can be heard on www.classwars.org. In addition, Fred has made a number of independent films (www.acornfilm.com).

Pilot's Song

Up at night and out to my graveyard,
Standing in the moonlight sleek and hard.
They strap me in and set great wheels a' rolling.
My body's pressed as from this earth I'm stolen.

Light is born so silent and sublime,
Delivered from the crescent womb of time.
And soon the east's aflame with day's desire,
To sow life's seed and to all things be sire.

The time is now, my dials won't be denied.
The air is thin; there's no place I can hide.
Down below, red death awaits my hand.
A thousand trembling bodies hug the land.

My gates are wide; I rise now to the sun,
Free from all the senseless blood to run.
And I thank the lord that I can't smell those fires;
Because burning bodies make heroes into liars.

CHORUS:

Ten miles high and I want to sing.
Sunshine on my silver wing.
There's earth below where I'm bound to lie,
For burning the children from the sky.

For Brian Wilson

This stops a trainload of bullets,
Destined for Central American hearts.

Now there is blood on the heavy wheels,
And a man gives his legs for peace.
Oh shame for those who stand upright,
And pay for murders out of sight.

Fourth of July

Ideals that inspired us two hundred years ago.
We fought for life and liberty,
And died to make it so.

But now these words ring hollow:
We've unleashed our war machine.
There's nary life nor liberty,
Where stars and stripes are seen.

War of the Ants

Their round, brown bodies twinkling in the sun,
They came together, not like one of Marlborough's victories,
But in a chocolate flow.

On my knees above the patch, I tried
To make out warriors or lovers.
But so small the ants, and teeming,
That their frenzy blurred their meaning.

Hours later, sun slanted low,
I surveyed again the field below.
Legless, the few that lingered there,
Writhed to follow, I know not where.

Ron Thomson is a US Army veteran who served in Vietnam in 1966 – 1967 with the Ninth Infantry Division. An avid long distance runner, in 1990 he and other Vietnam vets joined Soviet Afghanistan veterans in the Moscow Marathon, a friendship run through the streets of Moscow. *"There's a feeling of friendship here. Their problems from fighting in an unpopular war are very similar to what we Vietnam veterans went through when we came home."* He graduated from the School of Visual Arts in New York City majoring in the illustrative arts. Today he works as a full-time artist and gives workshops and classes that focus on capturing light and using vivid color to express the joy of life and being an artist. He lives in Amityville, New York with his wife and two children.
Web site: http://ronthomson.net

Lieutenant Billy Flynn

Our first mission in the jungle was soon to
begin.
My first lesson in death, it came from Flynn.
He was my Platoon Leader, Lt. Billy Flynn.
He was a West Point man.
He said he was there to save,
help and defend the people in that wretched land.
Instead he was our first killed in the Republic
of Vietnam.
Our Company Commander was wounded.
He was the next in command
But, his life was ended at a snipers hand.
A bullet in the head!
He never got to make a stand.
He never got a chance to save the people and we
never saved the land.
If I sound a little bitter, try to understand
Too many, (like Flynn) died for nothing
In the Republic of Vietnam.

Sergeant Connors

Sgt. Connors is dead.
They pulled his tee shirt over his head
so we didn't have to look at his face
as we carried him out of that place
though bamboo thickets, over dense vines and
branches,
through palms and broad leafed jungle plants
first dodging bullets, then red ants.

Carrying...looking at that blood soaked shirt
covering the three bullet holes in this face.
Fabric, sinking deeply into those holes
That memory will never erase.

Thirteen hours, wondering, scurrying, stumbling
Tripping, ripping through the jungle in a erratic
pace
Looking for a Huey landing space
We found it that night at another company's base.

But Sgt. Connors, he's dead
With three bullet holes in his face
And all these years later that memory
Will never erase!

The Ambush

They shot them dead
face down in the mud
all covered in blood.

Earlier our company received sniper fire
while we were on patrol.
So we left third platoon behind
To snipe the sniper
And show who was in control.

We succeeded in our mission
And put the snipers out of commission
As they were walking, laughing, joking, talking
With their rifles over their shoulders
We blew them away.
Turning both of them over,
We looked down in dismay.

Kids ... twelve thirteen if even.
I looked down and just had to walk away.
Killed, mutilated at such an early age
every emotion surfaced,
grief, sorrow, guilt, heartbreak,
pain, disgust, anger and then rage.

Kids... to them was just
A game.
Whoever sent them, must have been
insane.
Some of the men were so angered
They felt someone had to pay,
So they booby trapped their bodies
Before we walked
Away.

The Inauguration Day Waltz
Tune: "Columbus Stockade" by Charles B. Ward
("Casey Would Waltz with the Strawberry Blonde")

George, he will dance
With the girl he adores
While the war goes on.
They'll dance 'cross the floor
While Iraq is at war
And the band plays on.

Baghdad's exploded,
World relations eroded,
But he still shows no alarm.
He'll just dance across the floor
With the girl he adores
And the band plays on.

Our factories are closing
Their jobs they're outsourcing,
But he just goes arm and arm
'Cross the dance floor
With the girl he adores
And the band plays on.

Suicide bombings and roadside explosions
Our dead and wounded come home by the score,
But he'll just dance 'cross the floor
With the girl he adores
And the band plays on.

There's so much to care for
And so much to do for,
Medicare, Social Security and more,
But he'll just dance 'cross the floor
With the girl he adores
As the war goes on.

You voted for him
For a second term in
We'll all have to pay for your sins
As they dance cross the floor
Costing forty million or more
On a ball for supporters and friends!

Robert "Tack" Trostle enlisted in the U.S. Army after receiving his draft notice, and served in Vietnam, 1970-72. He has returned three times in the 90's to Vietnam to deliver medical supplies in the form of reconciliation. He is a member of Veterans for Peace and currently he lives and works in Lancaster, Pennsylvania. tackman02@yahoo.com

For Nguyen (Marie)

Thinking of her tonight
alternately smiling
and broken hearted.
Remembering her face
like it was yesterday.
A twenty year old memory
that still bathes me.
Maybe tonight
I'll feel her beside me
like many times before
but not hard enough to
make her reappear.
How could I let her go?

Maybe it was the war
that brought us together.
Both of us
doing what we had to do
to survive.
Was it love?
Or a relationship
of convenience?
A source of money?
A ticket to the States?
Temporary relief
from the lifers?
They say...
"Any port in the storm."
I never got to say
Good-bye.

The Price

Some say the price was too high.
Some, who used the resources of others,
would have spent more.
The price is paid in lives,
and limbs,
and minds.
It can be paid in an instant
without negotiation.
Or in installments
over many years.
The price is the inability to say
"Marine" or "Vietnam"
for more than 15 years.
A payment can be made
every July 16th
as you envision holding your best friend
dying in your arms.
There's the "Holiday Plan"...
tears in the shower
for no reason
every Memorial or Veteran's Day.
For me
The "Delayed Payment Option."
No payments for the
first 16 years.
The price includes titles,
taxes
and is subject to continuation
without notice.

WARNING!
THIS PRODUCT IS HAZARDOUS!
IT SHOULD BE DISCONTINUED!
IT IS NEEDLESS AND NONE OF
US CAN AFFORD IT.

10th Anniversary – "The Wall"

I feel like I'm doing it again.
Coming home.
Staring out the train window
into the darkness.
What's out there?
Other passengers are looking
me over,
thinking,
"Proud veteran?"
"Hero?"
"Baby killer?"
"Drug addict?"
"Crazy Nam vet about to go off?"

It's 20 years ago
all over again!
How many times
must I relive it?
How many times
can I?

Jose Vasquez has served fourteen years in the Army and Army Reserve as a Cavalry Scout, Medic, Nurse, and Health Services Instructor. In January 2005, he applied for conscientious objector status requesting immediate discharge from the military, which was granted in May 2007. Jose is an active member of Iraq Veterans Against the War (IVAW), serving as National Co-Chair of the Board and President of the New York City chapter. He is pursuing a Ph.D. in Cultural Anthropology from the City University of NY.

REVOLUTIONS

When we think of revolutions what are the images we see?
Are they images of men bearing flags and arms charging up a hill?
Is it machine-gunned palaces and gallows and burned out villages?
Do we see uniformed demagogues or marching militias killing and
burning and killing?

Or do we see somber bald monks seated and robed and connected?
Peaceful villages, broken weapons, happy children, no distinctions.
The revolutions I see take place in the mind
and begin with choosing peace

I AM WOUNDED TOO

I am a soldier
who survived the fear
of facing Uncle Sam
and saying Sir! No Sir!
I won't fight for lies
forgive me wounded soldier
for not being there
to ease your pain
I'll try on this end
to bring you home now

AMONG OUR MACHINES
(inspired by W.D. Ehrhart)

Among our machines
we feel invincible
crushing little brown
black, and yellow people
and sometimes white people

Among our machines
we can distance ourselves
from the killing
All we see is little
green men running across
our screens so we
shoot and cheer
when we get
those little fuckers
and reach the next level
of this video game
we call war

Among our machines
language and culture
become irrelevant
no need to talk
as long as we
can line up the cross-hairs
We drop bombs like rain
leaving scorched earth
and broken dreams

Among our machines
the mechanics of politics
rev up the engine
full throttle so we
can't even hear
ourselves think
And we don't
stop to ask questions
we just react
and kill to survive

Sam Weinreb was born in Brooklyn, New York and grew up in East Flatbush and Rockaway in Queens. He attended public schools in NYC that included Brooklyn Technical High School and graduated from Pratt Institute. Sam served in the US Army infantry, Germany, 1945-1946. He spent three years at the Art Students League and a decade in LA as a member of the Core Of Group Instant Theater. He was a faculty member at Parsons School of Design and set up their photo silkscreen department. Sam was fired for his involvement in organizing a faculty union and started making tofu in 1980. He writes poetry and is involved with Poets Against The War monthly readings at the Nyack Center in Nyack, New York. He is an active member of Veterans for Peace, chapter 60 in Westchester / Rockland, New York.

Sam wrote this poem in 2003 when he was out on a street corner protesting the war. *"...an illegal war and the fear and social hysteria beginning to infect our society..."*

Untitled 1

These are the times that fry men's souls
and heels.
The best lack all convulsions,
while the worst are filled with stale Coca-Cola.
The boundaries of Texas are unconstrained,
the Klu Klux Klan in white business suits
belly up to the oil tankers
and mate, creating bulbous SUV's
with an insatiable need for GLUB.
Oily CEOs smile and smile and smile,
then laugh out loud after filling their bellies at the trough,
the quality of mercy is unrestrained
if the military were restrained by global warming
it would quickly go away...

the military would make it go away.

WE HAVE TO DO BETTER!

Untitled 2

I stand on the dark street,
stare at my feet.
I used to be an ideologue,
jumping from certainty to certainty.

I have lived through ¾ of the last century.
Childhood through the Depression 1929 to 1941.
Adolescence through World War Two.
And then the glorious 50's,
Eisenhower and Nixon,
Lucille Ball and Desi Arnaz,
Ozzie and Harriet and Senator Joe McCarthy,
the beatniks and the standup comics,
the only resistance to blandness and intimidation, Interstate highways
and a mountain of white bread, Tip Top and Wonder Bread,
Nichols and May,
Second City, Shelly Berman,
Mort Sahl, Lennie Bruce,
Carl Reiner, Mel Brooks,
Sid Caesar, Imogene Coca.
And then rising out of the goop,
both Kennedys and Camelot,
Civil Rights, Martin Luther King assassinated along with Kennedy's,
Malcolm X and Medgar Evers.

The whole younger generation rises up,
Bob Dylan and Joan Baez,
hippies and yippies,
Abbie Hoffman, Woodstock,
the Beatles and the Rolling Stones.
Inner cities ablaze, Black Panthers
and Young Lords, Nixon in power,
Vietnam War over, China is contacted,
Watergate, Jimmy Carter,
then eight years of Reagan,
four years of Bush, then the Democrats,
under Clinton come to power,
but by becoming so moderate,
all but indistinguishable from Republicans.
Our politicians becoming more

and more like Macy's Thanksgiving Day balloons
and now daddy's boy is back, selected not elected,
the south rises in Republican garb,
good old boys with branding irons
and cowboy hats.
What's your beef?

But green grow the lilacs and Blake,
Byron, Shelly, Castaneda,
Emily Dickinson, Thoreau,
Walt Whitmam, e.e. cummings,
Kenneth Patchen, Kenneth Rexroth,
Lawrence Ferlinghetti, The Beats,
Alen Ginsberg, Gregory Corso,
Jack Kerouac, Leroi Jones,
sound their immortal yawp at official repression.
Wilhelm Reich rises from the ashes
to have us reclaim our generative vitality.
Culture is not something we approach on tip toe,
but something we make with our lives.
So let us hoist the green flag,
and dig in Mother Earth, planting seeds,
finding our roots in nature,
the good earth, fresh water,
clean air, and wholesome food.

Must everybody in the whole world eat at McDonalds?

Is that progress?

I don't think so.

That's my beef!!!

Jay Wenk served in the US Army during World War II as a rifleman with the Third Army in Europe. An avid bicyclist, he co-authored the book, *The Catskills: A Bicycling Guide*, that presents 27 tours in all parts of the Catskill and Shawangunk Mountains. He competes in the Senior Olympics. He works today as a fine cabinetmaker, and lives in Woodstock, New York, where he served as a Woodstock Town Board member and is President of Veterans for Peace, Catskill Mountain Chapter 058.

O-ver there...

Bodies of dead G.I.s
On the island beach
next to a sign
proclaiming,
"Kill The Bastards"
courtesy of Life magazine.
And that seemed good enough for me.
And so I went to do that.

They say,
we fought to save the world
From fascism,
O-
       there_____ ...
  ver

And now,
We say,
We fight to save ourselves,
ourselves.
To save ourselves and the world,
from fascism.
But not over there.

Dan Wilcox is a poet and photographer who is said to have the largest photo collection of unknown poets on the planet. Dan hosts the "Third Thursday Open Mic" for poets at the Social Justice Center in Albany, New York and reads poetry on a regular basis at various clubs throughout the Hudson River Valley. He is a member of a poetry troupe, known as "3 Guys From Albany." He is the author of *Meditations of a Survivor* (A.P.D. The Alternative Press for Albany's Poets) and has published eight books including two more of his own and a book for Anthony Bernini. He is an active member of Veterans for Peace, chapter 10 in Albany, New York.

THE BREASTS OF SQUEAKY FROMME
AWAIT BEHIND BARS

like those high school girls of my past
no longer too cute & perky
now as old as I am
heavier, thicker around the waist
– if still alive
perhaps with both breasts
womb intact, perhaps not
legs rounder, more blue
fannies flattened

you won't recognize me now
you didn't even notice me back then
so the question is
would I recognize you?

you're not my "great love"
now perhaps your pleasant smile
over dinner would be like salt
instead of that sophomore dance
I dreamed of beneath revolving lights
then our senior careers, each of us
drifting to our separate loneliness
away from holiday gatherings
Prozac wrapped in Dollar Store paper
meeting here like strangers on parole

A PAIN IN THE NECK

I wasn't able to go to the protests in NYC on August 29
the protests against the Republican National Convention
against George W. Bush & his right-wing agenda

I wasn't able to get on the bus that morning
with hundreds of others wanting more for working people
& less for the wealthy elite

I wasn't able to go to NYC to the protest
I woke up that morning & could not get out of bed
an electric spasm of tightening muscles
shot up my neck
& I wasn't able to turn my head

Or rather, I could turn my head, carefully
thoughtfully to the left, & I could look forward
but when I turned to the right, my body said "No"
an iron grip of pain forced me back to the left

As I sat all day over-dosed on aspirin
cooking under a heating pad
looking constantly to the left
feeling pain & restriction on the right
I thought of the protestors in NYC
& hoped the whole country would avoid
the muscle spasm of the right
& continue to look left -- & forward.

IF PEACE BROKE OUT TOMORROW...

If Peace broke out tomorrow
in this City, across our Country
throughout the World
would you be ready?

If Peace broke out tomorrow
would you be prepared
like they say we must be
prepared for War?

Would you be able to love
the "Huns", the "Japs,"
the "Gooks", the "Ragheads"?

If Peace broke out tomorrow
would you believe in Peace
as you believe in
the "Axis of Evil"
the "Weapons of Mass Destruction"?

If Peace broke out tomorrow
would you willingly send tax dollars
for schools & hospitals instead of
for bombers & air craft carriers?

Would you heed the call
from the Department of Peace
for volunteers, for Peacemakers
to beat swords into plows?

If Peace broke out tomorrow
like a flock of white doves
dropping olive branches on everyone
would you be ready?
Would you enlist?

("There is no way to peace – peace is the way." – A.J. Muste)

Larry Winters was born and raised in New Paltz, New York. He entered the United States Marine Corps after high school and served in Vietnam 1969-1970. Twenty-five years later, by then a licensed mental health counselor at Four Winds Hospital in Katonah, NY, he returned to Vietnam with other heath care professionals to study Post-Traumatic Stress Disorder (PTSD) in the Vietnamese people and to make peace with his past. Larry is a widely published poet, men's group leader and group psychotherapist. His new book, The Making and Un-making of a Marine can be purchased at his website makingandunmaking.com ,
as well as from millrockwriters.com.
E-mail: winters.lawrence@gmail.com
Blog: MakingAndUnmaking.blogspot.com

Vietnam

Cemetery Worker at Viet Cong Memorial

I called to you.

"Come here I have something for you."

You mumbled back.

I called again.

You mumble again.

I wave for you to come.

You looked away and spoke clearly.

"I no come here."

I wanted to give you money.

You who takes care of my enemy's graves.

But you turned away.

Both of us knowing it could never be enough.

America

"For all of you that live here during the Vietnam War ."
I killed for you.
You may not have asked me to,
but I killed for you.
I didn't ask to go to Vietnam.
I didn't support the war.

Still I killed for you and for me.
I killed for you,
while you paid your taxes.
You watched me kill on TV,
while you were eating cheeseburgers.
I killed for you.
While protesting that I was killing for you,
I killed for you.
While you avoided the draft,
while running off to Canada,
I killed for you.

You waited in the line at the supermarket,
you were out getting drunk,
you got your first good job after college,
you enjoyed free love,
While I was killing for you.
I have carried pain for you.
Guilt for you.
Shame for you.
For all the killing I did for you.
When I came home.
You expected me to heal for you.
To get on with my life for you.
To be productive for you.
To marry you.
To raise children for you.
And most of all to forget for you.

Confession

I'm ashamed that I may not have killed anyone in Vietnam.

I'm ashamed that I may have killed someone.

I'm proud that I was Marine.

I'm embarrassed to tell anyone that I was in the Marines.

I grew up believing in God and country.

In Vietnam I lost my belief in God and I distrust anything my country tells me.

Vietnam was the most beautiful country I ever saw: vibrant colors, skies piled with cumulus clouds, beautiful women with silk black hair.

Vietnam was an ugly, blood drenched sweating inferno where women and children were at times weapons themselves.

Vietnam made heroes out of school-boys.

Vietnam made traitors out of scared boys who hated what they were told to do but did it anyway.

I wanted my father to be proud of me for standing up and fighting for my country.

My father never asked me anything about the War when I returned.

I missed my girlfriend and married her as soon as I got home.

I divorced my wife and for years could not father our child.

Dayl S. Wise was drafted into the US Army in 1969 and served in Vietnam and Cambodia in 1970 with the First Air Cav. He is a member of Vietnam Veterans Against the War and Veterans For Peace. He lives part time in the Bronx and Woodstock, New York with his wife, the poet Alison Koffler; Molly, a Labrador-pit bull mix and Six, a calico cat with a bad leg. He self-published a chapbook, *The Best of Post Traumatic Press 2000*, a collection of poems by veterans, and is the author of *Poems and other stuff* (Post Traumatic Press).
E-mail - dswbike@aol.com

Spilling Out

Spilling out of the apple.
Seeds upon seed upon seed.
Sperm upon sperm upon sperm,
impregnating women.

Things we leave behind.
Children by men,
really boys,
who go to war.
30,000 years spilling
out of the apple.
O Eve, O Eve...

An endless cycle of rape
Rape of women, peace, earth.
Stop, stop, stop,
keep your seeds,
not a drop
a drip,
a dribble,
a splatter
or a leak.

Cultivate your garden
Honor motherhood,
Earth,
Peace.

M61 Fragmentation Grenade
"squeeze (my lemon) 'til the juice run down my leg"

Led Zeppelin

Simple:
pull the pin,
release the jungle clip,
throw.

Can be thrown 40 meters by average soldier...
I'm told.

Light sheet metal body, olive drab,
single yellow band at the top,
Nomenclature and or lot number marking also yellow.
Total weight 16 ounces.
We carried four.

Explosive core, 5.5 ounces of Composition B Filler.
Fragments are produced by a serrated wire coil fitted to the inside of
the grenade body.
Like a lemon pulp's 8 to 10 segments,
pale-yellow, juicy, acidy, only most have a few seeds
Some are seedless.

ALTHOUGH THE KILLING RADIUS IS 5 METERS AND THE
CASUALTY PRODUCING RADIUS OF THIS GRENADE IS 15
METERS, FRAGMENTS CAN DISPERSE AS FAR AWAY AS 230
METERS.

Many who have thrown lemons are still waiting
for the explosion that never comes.

Room 304
Columbus Elementary – '61

Black board, slate black.
Lettering, yellow line lower case,
white upper.
p-i-g to proper line.
My p's mirrored
beautiful q's.
Miss Ray's cross,
no stares today,
disapproving looks,
that damn pointer.
Wood one with the rubber end.
The business end.

Smell of steam, radiator grumbles.
Years of melted crayons,
Jackson Pollock-inspired.
Blues, reds, greens, yellows,
They're all there,
inventing others on the run,
blue violet, turquoise, violet,
green yellow, blue green, pine
orange red, violet, brick
yellow green, yellow orange, lemon,
mixing like lava flows toward the floor,
then disappear without a trace.
Where did they go?

Wooden oak desks, five rows,
six deep, each with ink well hole,
never to hold intended bottles.
No permanent stuff,
can't be trusted, those snot-nosed 6 year-olds,
only no. 2 pencils,
erasers on end.
1" square brown gum eraser, BIG jobs
leaving mounds of eraser effluent on floor
like snow drifts blowing into the corners
up to the window,
out the door,

taking with it the fifth row,
in alphabetical order
flowing out to the playground,
swallowing up Mr. Kull's gym class.
Susan Palmeri's ponytail,
(the girl I fantasized about in middle school two years later)
floating by on the ever growing brown eraser shavings.
Down the street covering the Cape Cod houses
spilling over the Kensico Dam,
down to NYC,
filling up the subways,
finally spilling out into the East River only to...
reemerge in Vietnam with the fifth row and Miss Ray,
pointer in hand. *"No stars today, class,"*
writing down names with crayon-stained hand ...
going to call all your mothers,
you're in big trouble waving pointer.
Gathering those responsible in tow,
bellowing *"YOU'RE ALL STAYING AFTER SCHOOL"*
as the brown eraser shavings retreat back to the sea,
pulls out an American flag,
attaches it to her pointer,
and rides out on the crest of the retreating brown gum eraser wave.
retreating back to the good old USA while the NVA collects our crayons
and starts the long journey back north.

Grenadier

Another white boy
Second recon team
A Grenadier
different
Carried a thump gun.
Us, standard issue M16,
different, this cracker was in love.

For close support,
this single shot,
single barrel,
break barrel,
rifled barrel
large bore,
sawn-off,
shoulder fired *blooper*
put the hurt out.

A southern boy
An RA,
high school dropout
No prom for him,
No white tux, red carnation,
No girl on his arm.
737mm tall,
with a barrel length of 355mm
weight (loaded), 3Kg.
A large flip up sight situated half way down
the barrel,
with a basic leaf foresight fixed at the end
of the barrel.
The rear sight was calibrated up to 375 meters
in 25 meter intervals.
They made a good team.
Cute couple,
highly accurate up to 200 meters.
400 tops.

At the dance you unlock the barrel from the
receiver
and move the safety to the SAFE position.

Opening the barrel cocks the weapon.

Extraction occurs while you are cocking.

As you open the barrel,
the spring-loaded extractor withdraws the
spent cartridge case

She does not eject rounds automatically;
you must remove the expended cartridge case
or live round from the barrel.

With the barrel in the open position,
you insert a cartridge into the breech end of
the barrel.

You chambering.
You lock.
You fire as you pull the trigger rearward.

Shot out.

You release the trigger,
the hammer settles back slightly.

300 fragments at 1,524 meters per second,
lethal radius of up to 5 meters.

Later, your beloved *"Thump-Gun"*, was replaced,
superseded by the M203 40mm launcher,
fixed beneath the fore grip of the M16.

Broken hearted over your loss you were never the   same.
Stopped talking, making mistakes,
Getting into fights,
your racism surfaced, I'm told.
You just disappeared,
collapsing into your self…

Born in Georga, To die north-east Phuoc Vinh.

2007

Walking my dog while at war
For Molly

Saw you at the pound
that first time,
ears down,
picked on by others,
bite marked belly.
Knew you were the one.

A hunter,
killed a rat
that first winter
in the Bronx.
A chicken three years later
in Ulster County.
Alison left
forty dollars in
their mailbox.

Late at night,
everyone asleep
opening up that box
writing of decade's-old demons.
By my side,
looking up
your boxer, pit bull
block headed face,
your worried look.

In a war many years ago,
another world, life...
men, teenage killers
looked up at me with that same look.
Did they...you love me as a hunter,
top dog, squad leader?

We ate, eat,
drink, piss and shit.
We guard, protect and aid.
We track, patrol,
alert, pounce, attack and kill.

OK ...I'm back, girl.
Get the leash.
Let's close this box,
go out and smell those sweet
Pelham Parkway smells
we both have learned to love.

Stay close, my friend.
Let's be *bad*.

High school dropout men of medicine,
clumsily restoring bowels to mutilated abdominal cavities,
while muffling the screams of unbearable pain and horror,
with injections of morphine and empty promises of tomorrow.

Body bags, toe tags, and medevacs to graves registration.
Military escorts, flag draped-coffins
and devastated loved ones,
comforted only by a seven gun salute
initiating the trumpeter's final farewell.
Patriotism, nationalism, and Communism,
the angry gods of archaic religions
all demanding appeasement through human sacrifice.
. . . I've become an atheist.

Memories, daydreams, and nightmares
my constant companion
as I await the merciful dagger of Brutus.

The Centurion

Concertina, tanglefoot, trip flares,
pebble filled beer cans, and claymores.
81 mike mikes delivering daylight upon command,
used sparingly so as not to compromise our position.
As though they didn't know.

Sensing devices, listening posts, and starlight scopes
providing eyes that penetrate the darkness.
360 perimeter integrity, sectors of fire overlapping,
with the 60s standing ready
to saturate the likely avenues of approach.

M79s and LAWs for added firepower
and to cover any deadspace the terrain may impose.
Reserves in secondary positions
to respond to sapper penetration,
with the COM established
to coordinate and control the entire fiasco.

PRC25s, FDC, and azimuths,
with pre-registered targets
for quick and accurate H.E. and W.P.,
air bursts my favorite.
Phantoms and Puff
providing a downpour of nap and steel,
with red smoke to pinpoint the inferno.

Strategy to match the brilliance of Caesar.
But this is not the Gallic wars.
Does Charlie appreciate such tactical genius?
How could he, for we are the noble legions
and he the ignorant barbarian.

The board has been set, and, like pawns,
we await his next maneuver.
Ghostly shadows, silently probing and sniping,
hoping to fund a vulnerable jugular.

Endless nights, limitless horror,
and senseless deaths.

And when they benefit from the carnage no longer,
their yellow ribbon patriotism
and shallow concern
fade quickly to apathy and indifference.
The living refuse of war that returns
are heroes no longer,
but outcasts and derelicts,
and burdens on the economy.
The dead, they mythologize with memorials
and speeches of past and future suffering
and loss.
Inspiring and prophetic words
by those who sanction the slaughter
to those who know nothing of sacrifice.

I used to try to explain war
to help them understand and to know its horror,
naively believing that war was a deficiency,
of information, understanding,
discernment, and vision.
But being crazy has liberated me
allowing me to see that war is not a deficiency at all,
but an excess, of greed, ambition, intolerance,
and lust for power.
And we are its instruments, the cannon fodder,
expendable commodities in the ruthless pursuit
of wealth, power, hegemony, and empire.

And now, I accept and celebrate my unorthodoxy,
my insanity, as an indictment
of the hypocrites and the arrogant,
of the ignorant and the narrow-minded
for a collective responsibility and guilt
for murder and mayhem,
and crimes against humanity.
And I offer my insanity as a presage
of their future accountability,
to humankind in the courts of history,
and to the god they invoke so often
to sanction and make credible
their sacrilege of war.

enjoyed the jazz, the excitement, the power.
They became avenging angels, even god herself,
making decisions of life and death,
but mostly death.
Those crazies hated to see the war end.
For me, the war never ends.

Sometimes things work out for the best, though,
as my unorthodoxy, my being crazy,
probably saved my life.
You see, sane people can't live like this,
in a war that never ends.
Not all crazy people can either.
Guess I was lucky.
Sometimes being crazy helps you cope.
Sometimes, I wish I was crazier than I am.

Serious introspection has made clear
the foundations of my unorthodoxy,
the nature of my insanity.
It is a cruel wisdom
Allowing no better, compelling
a clarity of vision.
I have seen the horror of war,
the futility and the waste.
I have endured the hypocrisy and arrogance
of the influential and the wealthy,
and have tolerated the ignorance and narrow mindedness
of the compliant and the easily led.
War's malevolent benefactors,
who pretend and profess their patriotism
with bumper-sticker bravado,
with word but not deed,
intoxicated by war's hysteria,
from a safe distance.
Appreciative of our sacrifices they claim
as they applaud the impending slaughter,
sanctioning by word, or action, or non-action
sending other men and women
to be killed, and maimed,
and driven crazy by war.

War Crazy

I have always thought myself a free spirit,
A philosopher mendicant,
seeking an alternative,
more substantive, lifestyle.
So many others, however, see my unorthodoxy,
my "spiritual seeking,"
as abnormal and a clear indication of my insanity.
Perhaps I need to pause and to reevaluate my life.
After all, being insane is not something one readily admits.
I guess it's part of being crazy
to cling to a facade of sanity,
to think oneself normal
and everyone else insane.

One thing I am certain of, however.
I haven't always been crazy.
Wasn't born crazy.
I think insanity crept up on me,
happened in Vietnam, in the war.
War does that, you know, drives people crazy.
Shell shock, battle fatigue,
soldier's heart, PTSD.
All that killing and dying can make anyone crazy.

Some survive war quite well, they tell me.
Many even benefit from its virtues.
But war's effects are not always apparent.
No one escapes war unscathed,
In body and in mind.
All war, any war, every war,
Ain't no virtue in war.

I think, of those not driven crazy by war,
many were crazy already.
But theirs was an insanity of a different kind,
a hard kind, an uncaring kind.
I knew people like that.
While I didn't like them much,
I thought them fortunate,
as killing and dying meant nothing.
In fact, in a perverse way, they enjoyed it,

Camillo "Mac" Bica, Ph.D., is a professor of philosophy at the School of Visual Arts in New York City. As a veteran recovering from his experiences as a United States Marine Corps officer during the Vietnam War, he founded, and coordinated for five years, the Veterans' Self-Help Initiative, a therapeutic community of veterans suffering from post traumatic stress disorder. He is a long-time activist for peace and justice, a member of Vietnam Veterans Against the War, and a founding member of the Long Island chapter of Veterans For Peace. Poems and articles by Dr. Bica have appeared in The Humanist Magazine, Znet, Truthout.com, Monthly Review Zine, Foreign Policy in Focus, and numerous philosophical journals.
E-mail: cbica@sva.edu
Web site: www.svaphilosopher.com

A Sign of the Times

A body of a dead VC sapper stands upright,
impaled in the layers of concertina wire
marking the no-man's land that surrounds
the perimeter of a firebase north of Danang.
Killed trying to penetrate the base's defenses,
his catatonic body adorned by holiday revellers,
with Christmas balls, tinsel, and a sign,
soiled with blood and entrails,
wishing all peace and good will
from Victor Charlie.
As we passed by and entered the base,
few even took notice.
I heard one young Marine,
nineteen years old and newly arrived in Country;
whisper to no one in particular.
"Ho, fucking ho, fucking ho."
We had grown indifferent to death and human suffering.
The innocence of youth dies quickly,
When killing becomes a rite of passage.

CONTENTS

ACKNOWLEDGMENTS

Some works in this collection have been published previously.

Marc Levy
poetz.com: (2006)   "AN OPEN DREAM TO RESIDENTS OF THE UNITED STATES"
New Millennium Writings: "He Would Tell You"

Michael Embrich
Helium.com: "I"

Larry Winters
makingandunmaking.com: "Confession", "Vietnam" & "America"

Gerald McCarthy
War.Literature: "Pylon" & "Winter Solstice"

INTRODUCTION
By Dayl Wise

I have put this book together to tell the stories of veterans with direct experience of the military. For some, the intense experience of war can only be expressed in poetry, while others are driven by the need to say something openly political. This chapbook includes veterans from World War II, the Cold War, Korean War, Vietnam War, peace time and the current wars in Iraq and Afghanistan.

Thanks to the soldier-poet contributors: Camillo "Mac" Bica, Richard Boes, Thomas Brinson, Michael Embrich, Michael Gillen, Marc Levy, Bob Lusk, Gerald McCarthy, Jim Murphy, Fred Nagel, Ron Thompson, Robert "Tack" Trostle, Jose Vasquez, Jay Wenk, Dan Wilcox, Sam Weinreb and Larry Winters. Some of these US veterans are seasoned writers, who have been published before. For others, this is their first time writing, their first time out crossing that line in public. Check out those who have web pages, blogs, myspaces and contact them by e-mail.

All works are poems, songs, short stories or spoken word with the exception of chapter 10 of Richard Boes' book *The Last Dead Soldier Left Alive*. (The book is his personal experience, a first hand inquiry into why thousand of Vietnam Veterans have committed suicide.) Richard's book can be ordered through booksellers or by contacting:

Iuniverse
2021 Pine Lake Road, Suite 100
Lincoln, NE 68512
www.iuniverse.com
1.800.Authors (1.800.288.4677)

Larry Winters' book, *The Making and Un-making of a Marine*, is his life's journey, which includes as part of its central theme the Viet Nam War and his search for a role in the world after the war, can be purchased at his website makingandunmaking.com.

Gerald McCarthy's book, *Trouble Light*- a new full–length collection of his poetry- will be published by West End Press/University of New Mexico Press in 2008.

Special thanks to Alison Koffler, Sharon Morrison, Dan Wilcox, Richard Boes and Jim Murphy for supporting me in putting this collection together. And to Gerald McCarthy who in 1993 signed his poetry book *Shoetown* for me. He also wrote the words, "...*write it out*"! I took his advice.